Countries Around the World

Canada

Michael Hurley

www.raintreepublishers.co.uk
Visit our website to find out
more information about
Raintree books.

To order:
☎ Phone 0845 6044371
▤ Fax +44 (0) 1865 312263
▣ Email myorders@raintreepublishers.co.uk

Customers from outside the UK please telephone +44 1865 312262

Raintree is an imprint of Capstone Global Library Limited,
a company incorporated in England and Wales having its
registered office at 7 Pilgrim Street, London, EC4V 6LB –
Registered company number: 6695582

Edited by Catherine Veitch and Charlotte Guillain
Designed by Steve Mead
Original illustrations © Capstone Global Library Ltd 2012
Illustrated by Oxford Designers & Illustrators
Picture research by Hannah Taylor
Originated by Capstone Global Library Ltd
Printed and bound in China by CTPS

ISBN 978 1 406 23534 0
15 14 13 12 11
10 9 8 7 6 5 4 3 2 1

British Library Cataloguing in Publication Data
Hurley, Michael
Canada. -- (Countries around the world)
971'.073-dc22
A full catalogue record for this book is available from the
British Library.

Acknowledgements
We would like to thank the following for permission to
reproduce photographs: The Art Archive p. 9 (National Army
Museum London); Bridgeman Art Library pp. 6 (Art
Gallery of Ontario, Toronto, Canada), 10 (Private Collection/
Peter Newark American Pictures), 29 (Art Gallery of Ontario,
Toronto, Canada/The Bridgeman Art Library); Corbis pp. 7
(National Geographic Society), 23 (Juice Images), 26 (Marie-
Reine Mattera), 31 (Bettmann); Getty Images pp. 8 (Stock
Montage), 11 (Hulton Archive), 19 (All Canada Photos/ Dave
Reede), 28 (Bryan Bedder); istockphoto p. 20 (© Roberto A
Sanchez); Photolibrary pp. 13 (All Canada Photos/Oleksiy
Maksymenko), 27 (Kristy-Anne Glubish); Shutterstock pp. 5
(© Niv Koren), 15 (© Pi-Lens), 17 (© kwest), 21 (© Keith Levit),
24 (© Zoran Karapancev), 25 (© Elena Elisseeva), 30 (© Debby
Wong), 32 (© GoodMood Photo), 35 (© Karen Gentry), 39
(© Helga Esteb).

Cover photograph of a train, Morant's Curve, Banff National
Park, Alberta, Canada, reproduced with permission of
Photolibrary (Tom Nevesely).

Every effort has been made to contact copyright holders of
any material reproduced in this book. Any omissions will be
rectified in subsequent printings if notice is given to the
publisher.

The publishers would like to thank Professor Emily Gilbert for
her assistance in the preparation of this book.

Disclaimer

Contents

Some words in the book are in bold, **like this**. You can find out what they mean by looking in the glossary.

Introducing Canada

What comes to mind when you think of Canada? Do you see the Canadian flag, with its red maple leaf? Do you think about big cities, or large areas of wilderness? Does it conjure up an image of the famous Canadian Mounties on horseback? Perhaps you have heard of the Great Lakes that stretch across the border with the United States?

Second largest

Canada is a relatively young country. It became a nation in 1867 after many years of war between British and French **settlers**. Canada is the second largest country in the world, and is part of the continent of North America. It has an area of more than 9,984,670 square kilometres (3,855,103 square miles) and only Russia is larger.

More than 33 million people live in Canada. People live mostly in the southern part of the country, near the border with the United States. Around 90 per cent of the population lives within 160 kilometres (100 miles) of this border. The northern part of Canada is very cold all year round and very few people live there. The **indigenous** people who do live there are known as Inuit.

Stunning scenery

Canada is an enormous and varied country full of stunning scenery, including dramatic coastlines, mountain ranges, glaciers, rivers, and lakes. Canada has approximately 2 million lakes! It is a country rich in **natural resources** such as oil, coal, gold, diamonds, and copper.

Surrounded by the beautiful natural landscape, people can have fun canoeing on one of Canada's many lakes.

History: conflict and change

Humans have lived in North America for around 20,000 years. Over time, these people settled all over Canada and what is now the United States. There were many different **tribes**, including the Huron and Dene.

These early tribes spent their time making tools and hunting for food. Coastal people caught fish, while the people living further inland hunted animals such as **caribou** and musk ox for meat. These **indigenous** people lived in this way for more than 12,000 years before any other **settlers** arrived in Canada. These tribes are now known as native Canadians, or First Nations.

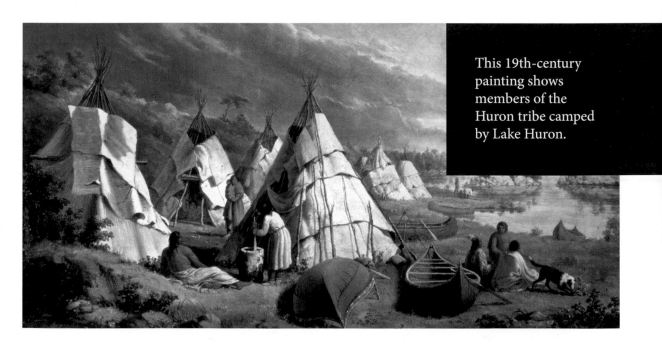

This 19th-century painting shows members of the Huron tribe camped by Lake Huron.

How to say...

The word "Canada" comes from the Huron and Iroquois word *kanata*. *Kanata* means village or settlement.

Vikings arrive

In AD 1000 Vikings from Scandinavia crossed the Atlantic Ocean and landed on the north-east coast of Canada. They set up a **colony** and gave it the name Vinland. The Vikings found the landscape on the north-east coast harsh and difficult to settle. They soon returned to Scandinavia.

Voyages of discovery

In 1497, an Italian called John Cabot, working on behalf of the English King Henry VII, set out across the Atlantic. He was an experienced sailor and **navigator**. He had planned to find a route to Asia, because at this time there was a valuable trade in spices. After a voyage that lasted nearly two months, he landed his ship on the eastern coast of Canada. Cabot named the area Newfoundland and claimed this new land for England.

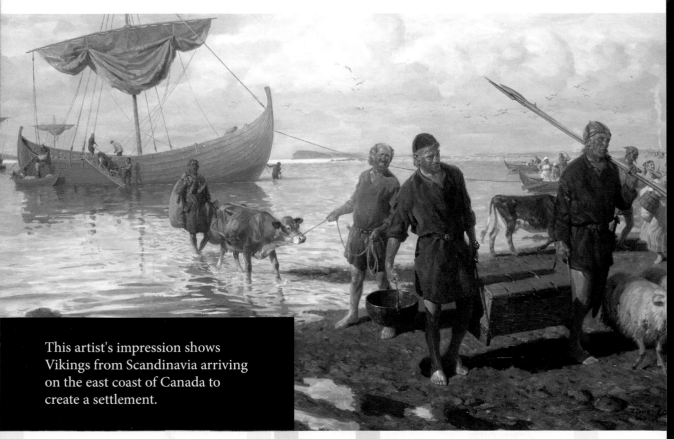

This artist's impression shows Vikings from Scandinavia arriving on the east coast of Canada to create a settlement.

"New France"

In 1524, France sent explorers to North America. First Giovanni de Verrazano travelled across the Atlantic, and then Jacques Cartier followed in 1534. In 1535, Jacques Cartier made a second voyage with three shiploads of French settlers to set up a colony. However, after a bitterly cold winter, many died, and the idea was abandoned.

The first Europeans to settle permanently came from France in the 1600s. They called the territory "New France". Samuel de Champlain founded Quebec City in 1608. The British also returned to Canada and set up their own settlements in different areas.

Conflict

There was rivalry between the French and British settlers, which led to many conflicts. The French and British were also fighting a war against each other in Europe. Battles took place on both sides of the Atlantic until the British defeated the French. Both countries signed a **treaty** in 1763, giving Britain almost complete control of Canada. In 1774, Britain allowed the area of Quebec to be administered by the French.

French sailor and navigator Jacques Cartier (1491–1557) made three journeys to explore the east coast of North America.

How to say...

English and French are the two official languages of Canada.

good morning	*bonjour*	(bon-jure)
hello	*salut*	(sa-loo)
bye	*au revoir*	(oh re-vwa)

The British and French also fought with and against native Canadians who were unhappy at the way their land had been taken. There were violent uprisings and many people were killed. The rebellion was stopped after Britain sent in more forces. Treaties were signed to bring an end to the conflict.

This artist's impression shows the British and French forces battling with each other for control of Canada in the 1700s.

Becoming a country

Between 1815 and 1850, Canada's population grew to around 800,000. These people came mainly from Britain, and settled across the country. Massive areas of forest were destroyed to create farmland for these settlers. The settlers built a basic **infrastructure** of roads and canals to transport people and goods. In 1867, the different colonies united and became one country: Canada. Canada's first **constitution** meant that there was now a central government in Canada, with a House of **Parliament**, but each area was responsible for itself. These areas were called provinces. Over the next six years, another three provinces joined the **Confederation**, stretching Canada over to the west coast.

This seventeenth-century artwork shows how European settlers traded with indigenous people, mainly for animal furs. The furs were sent to Europe to be turned into fashionable hats and other garments.

Railways and the gold rush

Because of the huge size of the country, railways were needed to transport people and goods across the land more efficiently. A network of railways was built between the growing towns and cities. The transcontinental railway connected the west coast to the east and was completed in 1885.

In 1896, the Klondike Gold Rush began. A **prospector** who was searching for gold near the Klondike River in the Yukon found a large nugget of the precious **commodity**. The news soon spread and within two years around 100,000 people had set off in search of their fortunes. Around 40,000 of them completed the journey, but only a small percentage found any gold.

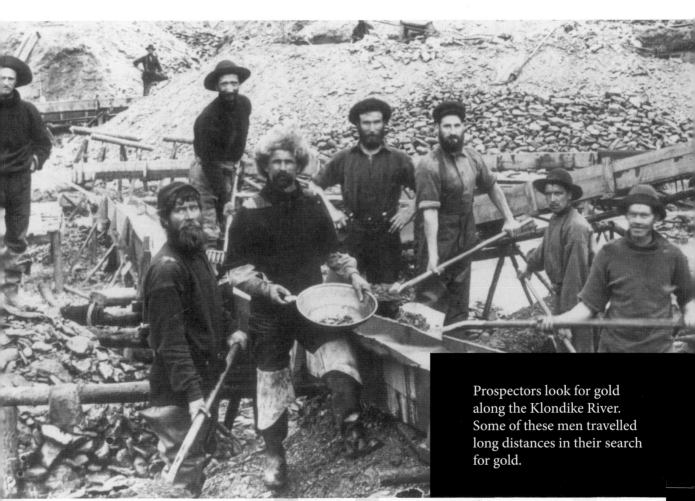

Prospectors look for gold along the Klondike River. Some of these men travelled long distances in their search for gold.

More fighting

During World War I (1914–1918) Canada sent hundreds of thousands of troops, many of them volunteers, to help the British and French fight against Germany in Europe. More than 60,000 Canadians died during this conflict.

Canada again fought alongside the **Allies** during World War II (1939–1945). Many Canadian troops were based in Britain. Again, Canada suffered devastating casualties, with over 40,000 soldiers killed in action.

Multiculturalism

After World War II, people from many parts of the world came to settle in Canada. Canada introduced an official **multicultural** policy in 1971. This policy aims to recognize and support the increasing **diversity** of the population.

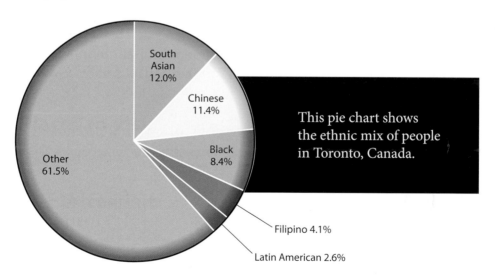

South Asian 12.0%

Chinese 11.4%

Other 61.5%

Black 8.4%

This pie chart shows the ethnic mix of people in Toronto, Canada.

Filipino 4.1%

Latin American 2.6%

KIM CAMPBELL (BORN 1947)

Kim Campbell became a member of parliament in 1988, and in 1990 she was the first woman to be appointed Minister of Justice and Attorney General. In 1993, Campbell became the first female prime minister in Canada's history.

Modern Canada

The Canada Act of 1982 ended British control of Canada, giving Canada responsibility for future constitutional changes. Although it had been mostly **autonomous** since 1867, this new act confirmed Canada as an independent, self-governing country.

For centuries, **immigrants** from other countries have settled in Canada. In recent times immigrants have moved to Canada from all over the world, particularly from Asia and the Middle East. They are attracted by the high standard of living, good quality of life, and opportunities for work.

Toronto is Canada's largest city and it is recognized as one of the most diverse cities in the world.

Regions and resources: land of lakes and mountains

Canada has a land border with only one other country: the United States. In the north-west of Canada lies the region of Alaska, part of the United States. The large island of Greenland lies in the ocean to the east of Canada.

Climate

Canada is mostly wet and warm on the west coast, while in northern regions the temperature hardly rises above freezing. People living in the southern part of Canada can experience very harsh winters. In the summer, this part of Canada enjoys a more **temperate** climate. The east coast of Canada does not get as cold as the rest of the country, but in the winter months the temperature is rarely above freezing.

This map shows the physical features of Canada, such as the mountains and rivers.

▲ Mount Logan

0   400   800 kilometres

0   250   500 miles

Hudson Bay

Key
land height above sea level:

- [ ] over 3000 metres
- [ ] over 1500 metres
- [ ] over 1000 metres
- [ ] over 500 metres
- [ ] over 200 metres
- [ ] below 200 metres
- —— country borders
- ▲ mountains

ROCKY MOUNTAINS

CANADA

St Lawrence River

N

Great Lakes

UNITED STATES OF AMERICA

Niagara Falls

Key landforms

The Great Lakes are five huge lakes that lie between Canada and the United States, with the national border running through four of these lakes. Lake Superior is the largest lake in the world. Niagara Falls, which is popular with tourists, runs into Lake Ontario. The Mackenzie River is the longest river in Canada.

The Rocky Mountains stretch from the north-west tip of Canada into the United States. In total, the mountain range is 4,800 kilometres (3,000 miles) long. The tallest mountain in Canada is Mount Logan, at 5,959 metres (19,551 feet). It is located in the Yukon Territory, close to the border with Alaska.

Daily life

In the winter, in the far north of Canada, the sun does not rise and the days are dark. In the summer, the sun never totally sets, so the nights are light.

This stunning natural phenomenon, which can be seen in Canada, is called the Aurora Borealis or "Northern Lights". It occurs when electrically charged particles from the Sun collide with atoms in Earth's atmosphere.

Territories and provinces

There are 13 different regions that make up Canada: 3 territories and 10 provinces. The three territories, Yukon, Northwest Territories, and Nunavut, are in northern Canada and cover a huge area of land. They are largely self-governed and the majority of the population in these territories is Inuit.

The 10 provinces of Canada are British Columbia, Alberta, Saskatchewan, Manitoba, Ontario, Quebec, Newfoundland and Labrador, Prince Edward Island, New Brunswick, and Nova Scotia. Quebec is the largest province and Prince Edward Island, off the east coast, is the smallest. Each province and territory has its own capital. The province of Quebec has a large French-speaking population. They have tried unsuccessfully to gain more independence from Canada.

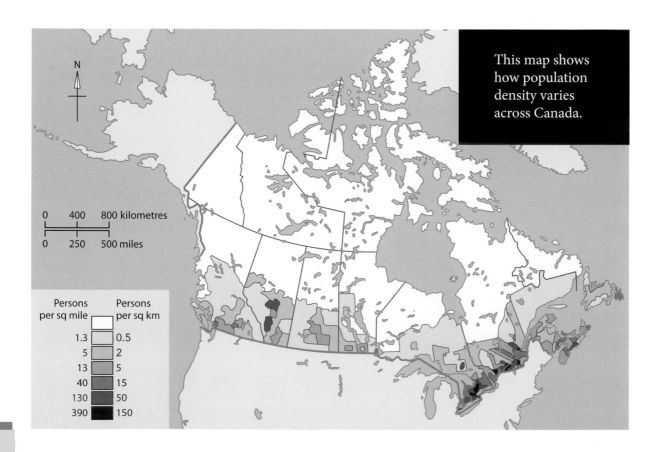

This map shows how population density varies across Canada.

| 0 | 400 | 800 kilometres |
| 0 | 250 | 500 miles |

Persons per sq mile		Persons per sq km
1.3		0.5
5		2
13		5
40		15
130		50
390		150

Major cities

The capital city of Canada is Ottawa, in the province of Ontario. Ottawa has a population of nearly 1.2 million people. Canada's largest city, Toronto, is also in Ontario, and has a population of around 5.4 million. The second largest city, Montreal, is in the province of Quebec, and has a population of more than 3.7 million. Canada's third largest city is Vancouver on the west coast of the province of British Columbia, with a population of nearly 2.2 million.

How to say...

The Inuit people who live in the Nunavut province have their own language called Inuktitut.

How are you?	*Qanuipt*	(ka-nwee-peet)
What is your name?	*Kinauvit*	(kee-nau-veet)
thank you	*qujaanamiik*	(coo-yam-na-mee-ick)
yes	*Ii*	(ee)
no	*aakka or aagaa*	(ah-ka or Ah-ga)
goodbye	*tavvauvutit*	(tah-vow-vo-teet)

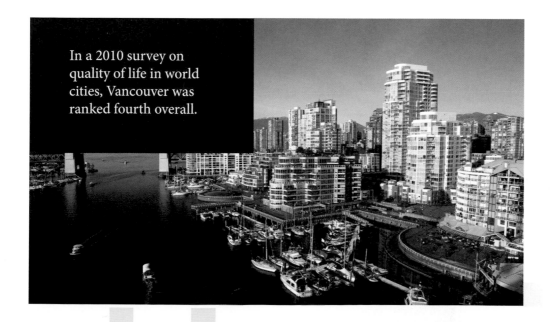

In a 2010 survey on quality of life in world cities, Vancouver was ranked fourth overall.

Economy

Canada has a strong **economy**. Traditional areas of employment include farming, fishing, logging, and manufacturing. The majority of manufactured goods are **exported**. In recent years, the government has invested in high-tech, modern industries. Modern technology also means that it is now very easy for people in **rural** areas to work from home.

Agriculture is also important in Canada. Wheat is the main crop, with nearly four per cent of the world's wheat grown in Canada. Other crops include potatoes and apples. Incredibly, 60 per cent of all Canada's agricultural goods are exported to the United States.

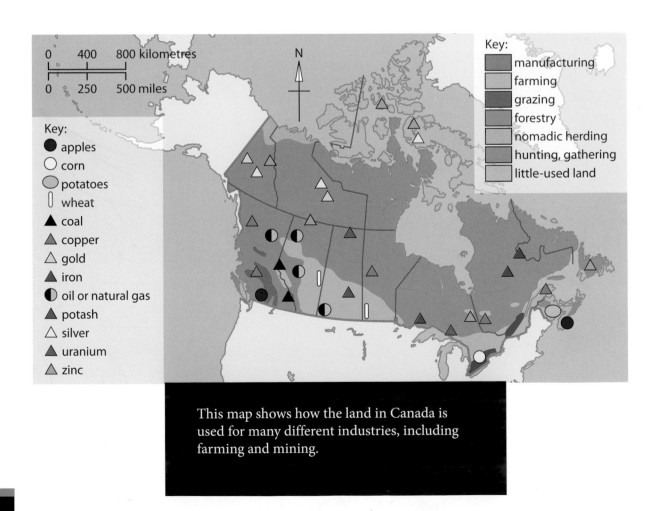

This map shows how the land in Canada is used for many different industries, including farming and mining.

A combine empties wheat into a grain wagon alongside it during harvest time.

Sustainability

In the Atlantic Ocean, off the coast of eastern Canada, stocks of cod fell dramatically in the 1990s because of over-fishing. In some areas, fishing was banned completely to allow the stocks to recover. New fishing techniques, including **fish farms**, have also been introduced to help stabilize the fishing industry. The timber industry is another large employer in Canada. It is important that logging is also carried out in a **sustainable** way. New trees must be planted as often as old ones are cut down.

Natural resources

Canada's **natural resources** include oil, natural gas, and coal. Canada also has iron ore, nickel, lead, copper, and zinc deposits which are mined. Eighty per cent of all Canada's mined resources are exported. This includes uranium and diamonds. Uranium is used in the production of **nuclear energy** and more uranium is mined in Canada than anywhere else in the world.

Wildlife: protecting nature

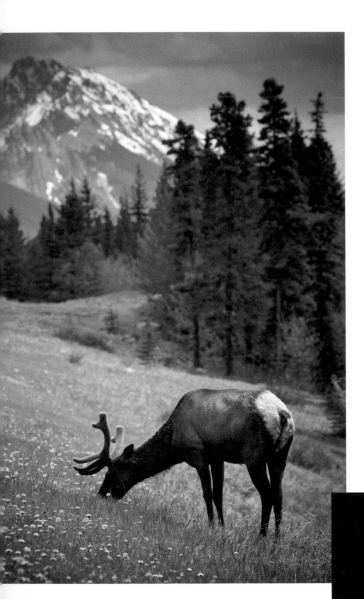

Canada has 39 national parks. Banff National Park was the first of its kind in Canada. Located near the Rocky Mountains, the park is 6,641 square kilometres (2,564 square miles), and the stunning scenery includes snow-capped mountains, glaciers, forests, and Lake Louise. The park is home to some of Canada's most famous wild animals, including **caribou**, wolves, and grizzly bears.

The smaller Forillon National Park is on the eastern tip of Quebec. It is a 244 square kilometres (94 square miles) landscape of steep cliffs, mountains, rivers, waterfalls, and forests. This protected area is rich in plant life, and 225 **species** of bird live or nest here, including jays, warblers, falcons, and owls.

The amazing scenery and glorious natural environment of Banff National Park.

Polar bear capital of the world

The small town of Churchill, on the edge of Hudson Bay in Manitoba, is the place to see polar bears in Canada. People travel from all over the world to catch a glimpse of polar bears in their natural environment on the vast **tundra** near by. When the ice freezes on the bay during the winter months, the polar bears spend all their time hunting seals. They need to eat as much as possible before the ice thaws and food becomes scarce.

Unfortunately, as climate change causes the temperature to increase, the time that the bears have to hunt on the ice is reduced. This is because the ice forms later in the year and melts sooner.

Some polar bears are so hungry that they walk into the town of Churchill looking for food. It is not uncommon to see a polar bear scavenging for food in bins.

The power of water and wind

Canada is the second largest user of **hydroelectric** power (HEP) in the world, after China. HEP uses moving water to create electricity and hydroelectric power stations generate the most electricity in Canada. The country has been producing electricity in this way for more than 100 years. HEP is an excellent way to create power because it doesn't harm the environment in the way that burning **fossil fuels** does. Canada has many rivers and lakes where hydroelectric power can be produced.

Wind turbines can also be used to create clean, **renewable** energy. Much like the way that HEP uses water to create power, wind turbines use the natural power of the wind to generate electricity. There are now areas called wind farms that have collections of large wind turbines. Smaller wind turbines can be used on farms and even houses to supplement electricity from other, more traditional sources. Using wind power helps to reduce energy costs.

Environmental damage

Canada has large mining regions where there have been major problems concerning the environment. The water and soil have become polluted and measures are now being taken to reduce this problem, and to prevent further damage. In certain affected areas, trees have been planted to reduce the flow of polluted water over land. Along with natural plants that absorb polluting materials, these measures have resulted in fish returning to previously damaged rivers and lakes.

Recycling

As the population rises, landfill sites in Canada are becoming full and new ones are needed to cope with the increase in waste. Recycling can help reduce the amount of waste entering landfill sites. Since the 1990s there has been a significant rise in the amount of recycling that is done, and households are now recycling more waste material than ever before.

This family are doing what they can to help the environment by recycling their household waste.

Infrastructure: leaders, health, and schools

Canada's government is a **constitutional monarchy**. This means it has a king or queen as **head of state** (Queen Elizabeth II), but the monarch's power is limited by a **constitution**. Canada is also a **parliamentary democracy**. This means citizens elect representatives. These elected officials appoint high-ranking politicians such as the **prime minister**.

Senate and House of Parliament

A general election is held at least every five years to choose a new government. However, elections often take place more frequently. The Canadian government has a Senate and a House of **Parliament**. The Senate is made up of 105 members who represent their area or region. The House of Parliament has 308 members.

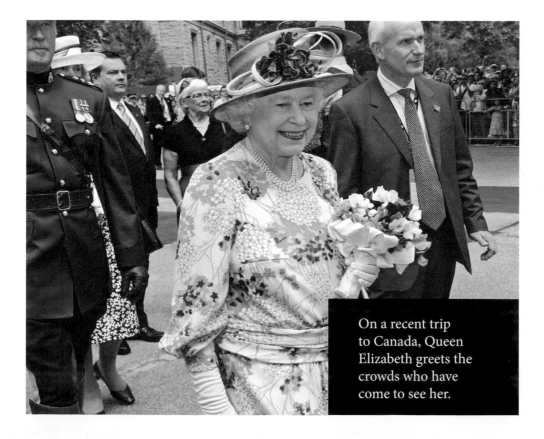

On a recent trip to Canada, Queen Elizabeth greets the crowds who have come to see her.

Member of the G8

Canada is a member of the **G8**, or Group of Eight. This group of industrialized countries, including the United Kingdom and the United States, meet once a year to discuss matters that affect global **economies**. The G8 representatives also discuss subjects ranging from climate change to diseases such as HIV/AIDS. Canada hosted the 2010 G8 summit in Huntsville, Ontario.

Healthcare

When people in Canada need to visit the doctor or go to hospital they do not have to pay. This is because they pay for their healthcare indirectly through taxes. In large cities such as Toronto, Montreal, and Vancouver there are modern facilities and hospitals. The standard of healthcare is very high.

Daily life

Because of the huge size of the country, getting to a doctor can be difficult in remote areas. People have to travel many hours to receive medical treatment. In emergency cases, helicopters are used to get people to the nearest hospital.

In this remote, mountainous region in the province of Alberta, a rescue helicopter is used to help people in emergencies.

School life

Each province and territory of Canada has control over its own school system. In most regions, pupils attend school for 12 years. In Quebec they attend for 11 years. Education is **compulsory** until the age of 15 or 16 in most areas.

A typical primary school day in the province of Nova Scotia starts at 8:05 a.m. and finishes at 2:05 p.m. Some of the children have breakfast at school. They have a 15-minute break, called recess, at 10 a.m., and lunch is at 12 p.m., for 30 minutes. Children have the option of taking a packed lunch or eating a school lunch.

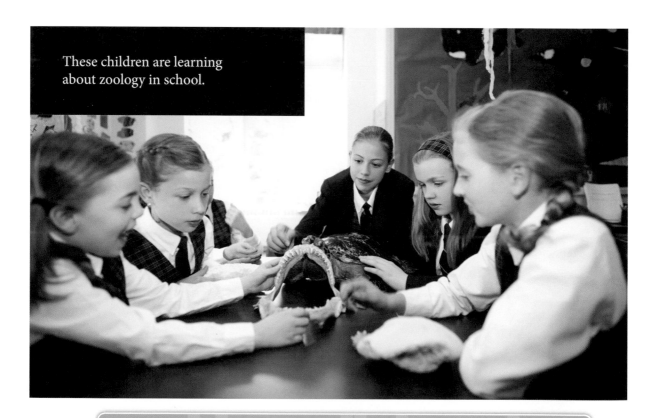

These children are learning about zoology in school.

YOUNG PEOPLE

Because Canada is officially **bilingual**, most students at school learn a second language. French immersion classes are quite popular across the country. At these schools, all classes are conducted in French.

Higher education

There are 95 universities in Canada as well as around 150 community colleges. Courses last between 12 weeks and 4 years. Some specialize in a certain area such as forestry, art and design, or Native studies.

Quebec has a **unique** education system. After secondary school, students spend two years studying at the Collège d'enseignement général et professionnel (CEGEP) before going on to university. Courses include social sciences and fine arts. Alongside their main studies, students must also take lessons in humanities, literature, and physical education.

How to say...

French	*le français*	(luh fronsay)
English	*l'anglais*	(longlay)
art	*l'art*	(lar)
history	*l'histoire*	(listwah)
geography	*la géo(graphie)*	(la jayo(graffie))
maths	*les mathématiques*	(lay mat-eh-mateek)
music	*la musique*	(la moozeek)

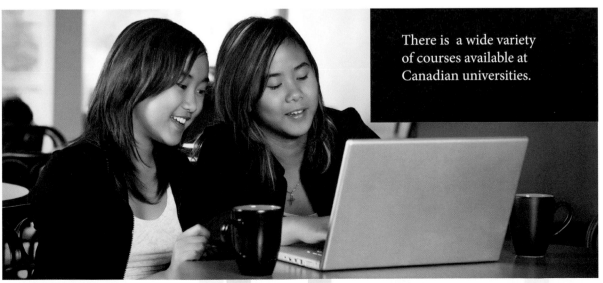

There is a wide variety of courses available at Canadian universities.

Culture: singers, stories, and Shrek

Justin Bieber performing in concert. He has fans all over the world.

The Inuit are internationally recognized for their traditional singing and dancing. Storytelling has also always been a big part of their culture. Stories have evolved over thousands of years and often involve spirits of the sea and land. The Inuit are very proud of their art. Many images are created using bright colours to depict different aspects of Inuit life, and the environment.

Music

Canadians listen to many different styles of music including rock, pop, jazz, and folk. World-famous Canadian music stars include Leonard Cohen, Joni Mitchell, and Neil Young. The Canadian singer Justin Bieber became a worldwide star after appearing on YouTube in 2008.

In recent years, several female Canadian singers have had international success. Shania Twain has sold millions of albums with her mix of country and pop music. Alanis Morissette and Avril Lavigne have had international number one albums. Perhaps the most famous Canadian female singer is Céline Dion. Her song "My Heart Will Go On" featured in the 1997 film *Titanic*.

GLENN GOULD (1932–1982)

Glenn Gould was a very popular and talented pianist. When he was only 15 years old, he performed in concerts, and he recorded his first album in 1955. He gave up performing in 1964 to concentrate more on broadcasting and recording.

Art: the Group of Seven

In 1920, seven artists decided that their art should have a **unique** Canadian style. They wanted to show Canada's beautiful **terrain** and rugged character. The group exhibited their art throughout the 1920s. The Group of Seven style is still very influential in **contemporary** Canadian Art.

Lauren Harris painted this image of lakes and mountains in 1928.

Film

There are many famous Canadian actors, for example Jim Carrey, Keanu Reeves, and Kiefer Sutherland. Many films are made in Canada because costs are cheaper than in the United States. Toronto is often used instead of New York City, as the two cities are similar in size, and have similar climates.

MIKE MYERS
(BORN 1963)

The comedian and actor Mike Myers was born in Scarborough, Ontario. He has appeared in the *Wayne's World* and *Austin Powers* films and is famous as the voice of the animated ogre Shrek.

Literature

Canadian literature is well-known around the world. Lucy Maude Montgomery wrote *Anne of Green Gables* in 1908. This story of a young **orphan** girl is set in the area of Prince Edward Island, which then became very popular with tourists.

The novelist Margaret Atwood has a loyal following of readers all over the world. She won the Man Booker prize in 2000 for her novel *The Blind Assassin*. The Sri Lankan-born Canadian writer Michael Ondaatje has also won this prize for his novel *The English Patient*, which became a hit film in 1996.

Sport

During the winter, Canadians like to ski, snowboard, and ice skate. Ice hockey is the most popular sport in Canada. Every town has an ice rink and major cities all have professional teams. These teams play in the United States National Hockey League (NHL). In 2010, Vancouver hosted the Winter Olympics.

During the rest of the year, many Canadians hike, canoe, and cycle around the country's rivers and lakes. Other sports that people enjoy are football, American football, and baseball. **Lacrosse** is the official summer national sport of Canada, while ice hockey is recognized as the winter national sport.

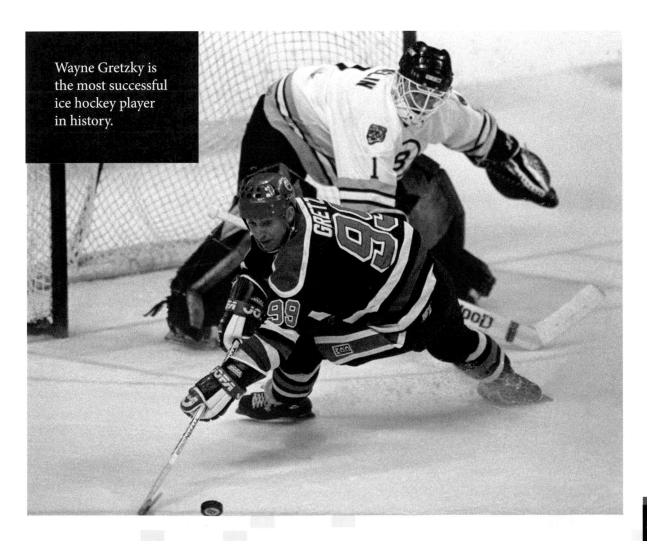

Wayne Gretzky is the most successful ice hockey player in history.

Television and the internet

Canadians have access to hundreds of channels on cable and satellite television. There are channels in English and in French. In 2009, 75 per cent of the Canadian population had access to the internet.

Food

Like people in most developed countries, Canadians have busy lives, and not everyone has time to cook a family meal every evening. Pre-prepared meals, fast food, and restaurants are very popular. The types of food available in Canada are diverse and have changed over time. In modern Canada, you can buy food from all over the world.

Canadians celebrate **Thanksgiving** in October. This is an important time when families come together and celebrate. Families cook a traditional meal of turkey, stuffing, cranberry sauce, squash, and potatoes. For dessert, there is usually pumpkin pie.

Maple syrup

One of Canada's most popular and famous foods is maple syrup. The syrup comes from the sap of maple trees, which grow in Quebec and Ontario. Native Canadians in the 1600s were the first to collect the sap, heat it, and transform it into syrup.

These buckets are used to collect sap from the maple trees. The sap is eventually turned into maple syrup.

Nanaimo bars

Ask an adult to help you make some delicious Nanaimo bars.

Ingredients – biscuit layer

- 100 grams unsalted butter
- 50 grams sugar
- 5 tablespoons of cocoa powder
- 200 grams coconut
- 1 egg (beaten)
- 250 grams crushed digestive biscuits
- 100 grams finely chopped almonds

What to do – biscuit layer

1. Melt the butter in a bowl over a pan of hot water.
2. Add the sugar and the cocoa powder and stir well.
3. Add the egg and stir until the mixture thickens. Remove from the heat.
4. Stir in the crushed digestive biscuits, chopped almonds, and coconut.
5. Press firmly into an ungreased 20 centimetre (8 inch) square tin.

Ingredients – cream layer

- 100 grams unsalted butter
- 2.5 tablespoons of cream
- 2 tablespoons of custard powder
- 400 grams icing sugar

What to do – cream layer

6. Cream the butter, cream, custard powder, and icing sugar together well.
7. Beat until light. Spread over the biscuit layer.

Ingredients – chocolate layer

- 100 grams dark chocolate
- 40 grams unsalted butter

What to do – chocolate layer

8. Melt the chocolate and butter over a low heat. Leave to cool.
9. Once cool, but still liquid, pour over the cream layer.
10. Chill in refrigerator until the chocolate layer has set.

Canada today

Canada is an ever-changing country, and its major cities are growing in size and population. The increase of **immigrants** from other countries has led to great **diversity** in cities. Tourism is, and will continue to be, important to Canada. People visit from all over the world to explore the cities and experience the wildlife and stunning landscapes.

Canadians love their sport, in particular ice hockey. They were especially pleased to beat their closest rivals, the United States, in the 2010 Winter Olympics in Vancouver.

Daily life

In the cold, harsh winters Canadians are able to carry on with their normal lives. In Montreal, for example, there is an underground shopping centre. This means the shoppers do not have to contend with the freezing conditions as they move between work, shops, and cinemas.

An important nation

Canada is a politically strong country. It is a member of the **G8** and the United Nations and works closely with other developed countries to find solutions to worldwide problems. Canada also has an important trade agreement with the United States and Mexico. This was set up to ensure that goods could pass freely across the three countries.

The future

Canadians are very proud of their country and many of them are passionate about the natural beauty of Canada. It is very important that a balance can be found when using the **natural resources**. The country's future development needs to happen in a **sustainable** way, making sure that the natural habitats of the country's wildlife remain undamaged for future generations.

Visitors from all over the world come to Canada to see Niagara Falls, which are amazing waterfalls.

Fact file

Official name:	Canada
Official languages:	English and French
Capital city:	Ottawa
Bordering country:	USA
Population:	34,030,589 (July 2011 est.)
Largest cities and populations:	Toronto (pop. 5.377 million); Montreal (pop. 3.75 million); Vancouver (pop. 2.197 million); Ottawa (pop. 1.17 million)
Urban population:	81%
Birth rate:	10.28 per 1,000 people
Life expectancy (total):	81.38 years
Life expectancy (men):	78.8 years
Life expectancy (women):	84.1 years
Ethnic groups:	British origin 28%; French origin 23%; Mixed 26%; Other European origin 15%; Other (Asian, African, Arab) 6%; Amerindian 2%
Religion:	Roman Catholic 42.6%; Protestant 23.3%; None 16%; Other Christian 4.4%; Muslim 1.9%; Other 11.8%
Internet users:	26.96 million
Military service:	voluntary

Type of government:	**constitutional monarchy**, **parliamentary democracy**
National animal:	Canadian beaver
National tree:	maple
Climate:	**temperate** in the south, subarctic and arctic in the north
Total area:	9,984,670 square kilometres (3,855,103 square miles)
Land area:	9,093,507 square kilometres (3,511,023 square miles)
Water area:	891,163 square kilometres (344,079 square miles)
Mountains:	Logan; St Elias; Lucania
Major rivers:	Mackenzie; Yukon; St Lawrence
Highest elevation:	Mount Logan 5,959 metres (19,551 feet)
Lowest elevation:	Atlantic coast 0 metres (0 feet)
Currency:	Canadian dollar (C$)
Resources:	iron ore; nickel; zinc; gold; silver; diamonds; fish; timber; coal; petroleum, natural gas
Major industries:	processed and unprocessed minerals; food products; wood and paper; fish; petroleum; natural gas; transportation equipment; chemicals
Main imports:	machinery and equipment; motor vehicles and parts; crude oil; chemicals; electricity
Main exports:	industrial machinery; aircraft; telecommunications equipment; plastics; fertilizers; timber; aluminium; uranium; wheat

Famous Canadians

Margaret Atwood (author); Donavon Bailey (athlete); Justin Bieber (singer); Joseph Armand Bombardier (inventor); Michael Bublé (singer/songwriter); Kim Campbell (politician); Jim Carrey (actor); Linda Evangelista (model); Wayne Gretzky (ice hockey player); Avril Lavigne (singer/songwriter); Cluny Macphearson (inventor); Mike Myers (actor); Anna Paquin (actress); Keanu Reeves (actor); Jacques Villeneuve (racing driver)

National holidays

1 January	New Year's Day
March/April	Good Friday and Easter Monday
May	Victoria Day
1 July	Canada Day
September	Labour Day
October	**Thanksgiving** Day
11 November	Remembrance Day
25 December	Christmas Day
26 December	Boxing Day

National anthem

"O Canada" was adopted as the national anthem on 1 July 1980. The music was composed by Calixa Lavallée, and the original French lyrics were written by Adolphe-Basile Routhier. The official English lyrics are based on a version written in 1908 by Robert Stanley Weir. They are as follows:

O Canada!
Our home and native land!
True patriot love in all thy sons command.
With glowing hearts we see thee rise,
The True North strong and free!
From far and wide, O Canada,
We stand on guard for thee.
God keep our land glorious and free!
O Canada, we stand on guard for thee.
O Canada, we stand on guard for thee.

Academy Award winner Anna Paquin is one of Canada's most famous actors. She is well-known for playing the character Rogue in the X-Men films.

Timeline

BC is short for "before Christ". BC is added after a date and means that the date occurred before the birth of Jesus Christ, for example, 450 BC.

AD is short for Anno Domini, which is Latin for "in the year of our Lord". AD is added before a date and means that the date occurred after the birth of Jesus Christ, for example, AD 720.

28000 BC	The first residents of what is now Canada arrive over the Bering Strait
AD 1000	Vikings arrive from Scandinavia
1497	Italian **navigator** John Cabot reaches the coast of Newfoundland
1534	Jacques Cartier explores the St Lawrence River and claims the shores of the Gulf of St Lawrence for France
1535	French **settlers** arrive to set up a **colony**, but many die during the winter and the attempt is abandoned
1583	Newfoundland becomes England's first overseas colony
1600s	Fur trade rivalry ensues between the French, English, and Dutch. The Europeans form alliances with some of the native people.
1608	Samuel de Champlain establishes a colony in Quebec and founds "New France"
1670	Hudson's Bay Company is established by British traders
1701	Forty First Nations chiefs sign a peace **treaty** with the French and the English, ending 100 years of war
1756	The Seven Years' War begins between New France and the larger and wealthier British colonies. After early French successes, the settlement of Quebec falls in 1759, and the British advance on Montreal.
1763	Britain is given almost complete control of Canada
1774	The Quebec Act recognizes the French language and the Roman Catholic religion in the colony. France is given administrative control of Quebec.

1791	Quebec is divided into Lower Canada (present-day Quebec) and Upper Canada (present-day Ontario) to form the province of Canada
1818	The 49th parallel becomes accepted as the border between the USA and Canada
1857	Ottawa becomes the capital of the province of Canada
1867	The provinces, including Ontario, Quebec, Nova Scotia, and New Brunswick, unite to become Canada. John A. Macdonald becomes the first **prime minister.** Over the next six years, the provinces of Manitoba, British Columbia, and Prince Edward Island are also included.
1885	The Canadian-Pacific railway is completed
1896–1898	The Klondike Gold rush ensues along the upper Yukon River
1914	World War I begins. Canada fights on the side of Britain and France.
1939	World War II begins. Canada fights again on the side of Britain and France.
1949	Newfoundland joins Canada
1965	The present Canadian flag is adopted
1971	The **Multicultural** Policy is declared
1980	"O Canada" is proclaimed as Canada's national anthem, 100 years after it was first sung on 24 June 1880
1982	The Canada Act and **Constitution** Act are signed, giving Canada control over future constitutional changes
1991	Canadian forces participate in the Gulf War following Iraq's invasion of Kuwait
1992	The leaders of Canada, the USA, and Mexico agree to the terms of the North American Free Trade Agreement (Nafta)
1993	Kim Campbell becomes the first female prime minister
1995	A referendum in Quebec rejects independence by a margin of only 1 per cent
1999	The territory of Nunavut is formed in northern Canada
2010	Canada hosts the Winter Olympics in Vancouver and the **G8** summit in Huntsville, Ontario

Glossary

Allies group of countries that fought together during World War II, including the United Kingdom, France, and Canada

autonomous mainly self-governed

bilingual able to speak two languages

caribou large deer

colony country ruled by another country

commodity something of use or value

compulsory when there is a requirement to do something

confederation union of areas to become one

constitution system of principles by which a country is governed

constitutional monarchy system of government in which a monarch (king or queen) is the head of state, but his or her power is restricted by a constitution

contemporary something that is of the present time

diversity having many different kinds or forms

economy all the produce and trade of a country

export sell goods to another country

fish farm business where fish are bred and reared in captivity for selling as food

fossil fuel combustible organic material, such as coal or oil

G8 group of wealthy nations, including Canada, the United Kingdom, and the United States that meet every year to discuss issues affecting global economies, as well as issues such as disease and climate change

head of state person who is the chief representative of a country

hydroelectric electricity produced by water power

immigrant person who comes to live permanently in a foreign country

indigenous originating in a particular place

infrastructure basic framework of a country, such as government and schools

lacrosse game in which two 10-member teams try to hit a small ball into each other's netted goal. Each player has a stick with a netted pocket for catching, carrying, or throwing the ball.

multicultural representing many different cultures

natural resource naturally occuring material that people can use

navigator person who explores by sea

nuclear energy energy released from the centre of atoms

orphan child whose parents have both died

parliament ruling body of some countries; laws are made there

parliamentary democracy system of government in which citizens elect representatives, and these representatives, in turn, appoint high-level politicians such as the prime minister

prime minister head of a parliamentary government

prospector person who searches or explores for something valuable, such as gold

renewable able to be used over and over again without any loss of resources

rural having to do with the country

settler someone who moves to a country and establishes themselves there

species type of animal, bird, or fish

sustainable using a resource in a way that means it is not permanently damaged or depleted

temperate neither very hot nor very cold

terrain area of land that has natural features

Thanksgiving second Monday in October, observed in Canada as a public holiday and the day for giving thanks for the year's harvest

treaty formal agreement between two states

tribe group of people who are linked by common ancestry

tundra huge area of treeless plain in the Arctic

unique only one of its kind

Find out more

Books

Fiction

Anne of Green Gables, L.M. Montgomery (Puffin Classics)

Underground to Canada, Barbara Smucker (Puffin, 2009)

Non-fiction

Crazy about Canada!: Amazing Things Kids Want to Know, Canadian Geographic Kids Books, (Maple Tree Press, 2006)

National Geographic Countries of the World: Canada, Brian Williams (National Geographic Society, 2009)

The Big Book of Canada: Exploring the Provinces and Territories, Christopher Moore (Tundra Books, 2003)

The Kids Book of Canada, Barbara Greenwood (Kids Can Press, 2007)

DVDs

Anne of Green Gables, Megan Fellows, Colleen Dewhurst, and Richard Farnsworth (Sullivan Entertainment, 2002) Classification: U

Websites

kids.nationalgeographic.com/kids/places/find/canada/

This website has games, videos, and articles all about Canada.

kids.yahoo.com

Type "Canada" into this search engine and find lots of photos, videos, and articles, as well as links to other great sites about Canada.

www.canadiangeographic.ca/kids/

You can find animal facts, games, maps, and more here!

Places to visit

If you are fortunate enough to visit Canada, here are some of the places that you could visit:

Niagara Falls, Ontario

A visit to the world famous natural wonder of the Niagara Falls is a great way to start exploring the Great Lakes.

CN Tower, Toronto

One of the tallest towers in the world, CN Tower dominates the Toronto skyline. High speed lifts take you to the top of the tower where you can look out across the city in all directions.

Kluane National Park and Reserve of Canada

Visitors to this National Park can catch a glimpse of grizzly bears and black bears in their natural environment. The Park is also home to Canada's tallest peak, Mount Logan.

Watch a live ice hockey match

You can watch a professional ice hockey match in every major city in Canada.

Topic tools

You can use these topic tools for your school projects. Trace the map on to a sheet of paper, using the thick black outline to guide you.

The Canadian flag, with a big red maple leaf, was made the official flag of Canada in 1963. Copy the flag design and then colour in your picture. Make sure that you use the right colours!

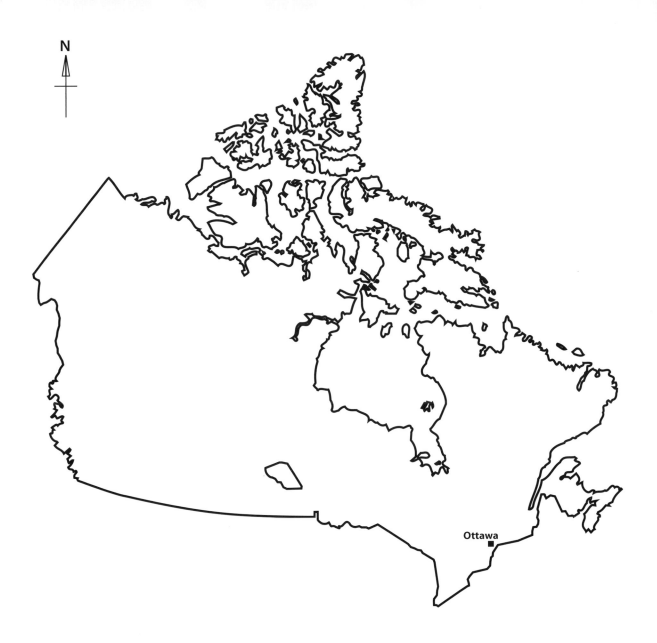

N

Ottawa

Index

Titles in the series

Afghanistan	978 1 406 22778 9	Japan	978 1 406 23548 7
Algeria	978 1 406 23561 6	Latvia	978 1 406 22795 6
Australia	978 1 406 23533 3	Liberia	978 1 406 23563 0
Brazil	978 1 406 22785 7	Libya	978 1 406 23564 7
Canada	978 1 406 23534 0	Lithuania	978 1 406 22796 3
Chile	978 1 406 22786 4	Mexico	978 1 406 22790 1
China	978 1 406 23547 0	Morocco	978 1 406 23565 4
Costa Rica	978 1 406 22787 1	New Zealand	978 1 406 23536 4
Cuba	978 1 406 22788 8	North Korea	978 1 406 23549 4
Czech Republic	978 1 406 22792 5	Pakistan	978 1 406 22782 6
Egypt	978 1 406 23562 3	Philippines	978 1 406 23550 0
England	978 1 406 22799 4	Poland	978 1 406 22797 0
Estonia	978 1 406 22793 2	Portugal	978 1 406 23578 4
France	978 1 406 22800 7	Russia	978 1 406 23579 1
Germany	978 1 406 22801 4	Scotland	978 1 406 22803 8
Greece	978 1 406 23575 3	South Africa	978 1 406 23537 1
Haiti	978 1 406 22789 5	South Korea	978 1 406 23551 7
Hungary	978 1 406 22794 9	Spain	978 1 406 23580 7
Iceland	978 1 406 23576 0	Tunisia	978 1 406 23566 1
India	978 1 406 22779 6	United States of America	978 1 406 23538 8
Iran	978 1 406 22780 2	Vietnam	978 1 406 23552 4
Iraq	978 1 406 22781 9	Wales	978 1 406 22804 5
Ireland	978 1 406 23577 7	Yemen	978 1 406 22783 3
Israel	978 1 406 23535 7		
Italy	978 1 406 22802 1		